Photo By *Grabill*
A LEGACY OF IMAGES

Burch and Bill Grabill's Northwest Louisiana

Presented by:
Noel Memorial Library
Archives and Special Collections
LSU in Shreveport

Photo selection and captioning:
Laura Street Conerly, Archivist
Noel Memorial Library, LSU in Shreveport

Researchers:
Domenica Carriere and Glenda Sharbono,
Noel Memorial Library, LSU in Shreveport

Text:
Robert Miciotto,
Noel Memorial Library,
LSU in Shreveport

Copyright© 2003 • ISBN: 1-932129-53-7

Published by Pediment Publishing, a division of The Pediment Group, Inc. www.pediment.com   printed in Canada

Contents

Foreword

THIS VOLUME IS DEVOTED to a photographic celebration of the work of two of Shreveport's most important and gifted photographers, father and son, Burch and William Grabill. The bulk of their professional legacy of photographic negatives and prints, generously donated by the Grabill family to LSU in Shreveport's Noel Memorial Library Archives, probably represents the largest and most important visual documentation of Shreveport and area history of the twentieth century. In chronological sweep and professional variety–in portraiture, as well as in social, commercial, aerial and photojournalistic photography, this work is locally unequaled. Indeed, the result of their diverse and considerable photographic efforts, which encompassed more than eight decades, is an unsurpassed visual legacy of area social and cultural history.

The vast majority of the approximately two hundred images selected for this volume have been carefully chosen from the numerous negatives and prints which form the substance of the Grabill Collection. In fact, the collection itself consists of over thirty-five hundred negatives and some one hundred prints. From this number, an attempt was made to gather the most historically relevant and visually appealing examples of their work from each of their Shreveport decades. A few Grabill photographs from previous publications were simply too good and appropriate to be left out, although, the majority of the images in this volume are previously unpublished. For the elder Burch Grabill, the time frame was extended to include examples of his work prior to the family's arrival in Shreveport in 1919. This meant inclusion of photographs from his Fayetteville, Arkansas years as a studio, field, and university photographer, and also for the relatively short period during World War I when Grabill was the military photographer for Camp Beauregard in Central Louisiana.

An additional and important aid to this effort which needs to be acknowledged is a 1993 series of Bill Grabill oral interviews conducted by former LSU in Shreveport archivist, Stephen J. Hussman. They have been an invaluable source of information about the man and his career. The result of this assembly of materials is a five-chaptered compilation of photographs and text with an historical arc which extends from the late nineteenth to the last decades of the twentieth century.

The staff of the Noel Memorial Library Archives is particularly pleased to be able to gather and bring to the public this trove of historical photographs. The Archives itself serves as the major research center for the history of the Red River region of Northwest Louisiana and, since 1975, has become the preeminent repository of the documents, images, and artifacts of regional history, which form the core of its over 560 collections. To that number can now be added another prized collection available for researchers, that underscores and furthers its mission of enhancing the historical knowledge and understanding of Shreveport and the surrounding area.

— *Laura Street Conerly, Robert Miciotto*
Noel Memorial Library, LSU in Shreveport

GRABILL
#3291

The Early Years

BURCH ENOS GRABILL WAS BORN IN 1871 in the small east central Indiana town of Pennville. Orphaned in his youth, he was raised by relatives and early-educated in the public schools of Indiana and neighboring Ohio. Very little is actually known of his youth and early adulthood, and according to his son Bill, it is a period of which his father only reluctantly and seldom spoke. It is known that by 1890 he lived in Wilmington, Ohio, and in that year entered Wilmington College, a small Quaker school that offered him both collegiate preparatory and regular college classes. Evidently while acquiring an education in the liberal arts with an emphasis in the sciences, Grabill's interest was aroused by the possibility of photography as a profession. In any event, it was in the period that immediately followed his years at Wilmington College (1890-1894) that he and a friend attempted to establish themselves as professional photographers in the little Indiana town of Gas City. Whether or not this venture was commercially successful is unknown, in fact, its lack of success may have encouraged his decision in 1898 to volunteer for military service in the Spanish-American War. As a twenty-six-year-old military photographer, Corporal Grabill was sent to the Philippines where he not only plied his trade for the army but was also involved in combat. Shortly after this one-year conflict was over, he returned to his hometown of Pennville before deciding to seek his future in photography further south in Fayetteville, Arkansas in 1901.

Now in his early thirties, Burch Grabill was about to enter a professionally positive phase in his career. What precisely motivated this Midwesterner to settle in Northwest Arkansas is uncertain, surely paramount was the promise of vocational success. In short order, he secured a studio on the west side of the Fayetteville town square and also became the official photographer for the University of Arkansas, a position he maintained until he left the city some fifteen years later. During this era, which lasted from 1901 to 1916, Grabill was robustly engaged in

Above: Burch Grabill with son, William.

Opposite: Burch Grabill in his darkroom, Fayetteville, Arkansas.

Right: William,
Fletcher and mother,
Maude Davis Grabill.

his work, and has left a rich legacy of photographs from the Fayetteville years—scenes of campus, countryside, and city, as well as studio portraits.

It was also during his years in Arkansas that Grabill married and began his family. At the time of their marriage, Maude Averill Davis was a twenty-five-year-old music teacher from Springdale, Arkansas, a town located a few miles north of Fayetteville. They were wed in October 1903, had their first son, Wilson Fletcher, in 1909, and their second and last child, William Burch Grabill, in 1913. In the years ahead, Maude Grabill very much became the professional aide of her husband and even later,

Above: University of Fayetteville coeds on an outing in Fayetteville Square, ca. 1911. Grabill Studio in background. *University of Arkansas, Special Collections.*

Above: Fayetteville, Arkansas City Directory cover. Advertisement for Grabill Studio, cover page, 1904. *University of Arkansas, Special Collections.*

Left: University of Arkansas, campus scene showing Peabody and Carnall Halls framing "The Lonesome Pine," 1914. *Picture Collection 4048, University of Arkansas, Special Collections.*

U of A Cadets parading on Armistice Day, November 11, 1918 on Public Square, Fayetteville, Arkansas. World War I

Above: University of Arkansas cadets parading, Armistice Day, Fayetteville Square, Fayetteville, Arkansas, Nov. 11, 1918. Though no longer living in Fayetteville, the Grabills returned on a regular basis to their farm and maintained a connection with the University for many years. *University of Arkansas, Special Collections, Campbell Photo Albums & Papers, MC1427.*

after his death in 1936, maintained the same role of more than occasional studio photographer and active co-owner of the business with her younger son, Bill. The Grabill family was very fond of the Fayetteville area, and even after moving away, continued to own and enjoy their 25 acre farm and vineyard on nearby Mount Sequoyah into the 1930s, well over a decade after their departure south to Louisiana.

In 1916, in anticipation of United States involvement in the First World War, Grabill was able to secure a position as the military photographer for Camp Beauregard in Rapides Parish in Central Louisiana, just northeast of Alexandria, near Pineville. Here on the campgrounds he maintained a studio and engaged in an assignment in some ways reminiscent of his Spanish-American War experience as a government-employed photographer. Unfortunately, very few examples of Grabill's work from this time have been found. During this three-year period, the Grabill family

Above: Camp Beauregard, Pineville, Louisiana, barracks, ca. 1917.

Below: Burch Grabill with R. B. Cyclegraphic camera made by Eastman Kodak. This camera was capable of making a 360 degree photograph. Camp Beauregard, Pineville, Louisiana, ca. 1916.

Above: Camp Beauregard, Pineville, Louisiana, training field, ca. 1917.

Photo By Grabill ~ 9

Right: Morris & Dickson Co., 220-222 Travis Sreet, 1919.

Below: Caddo Parish Courthouse Square, 1919.

lived in Alexandria in a home not too distant from Red River, and opened a second smaller studio in the city itself.

With the end of the hostilities of the War in November 1918 and the conclusion of the Camp

Beauregard years, the Grabills were faced with the prospect of finding a new home. A short interlude of uncertainty followed until the elder Grabill decided that the burgeoning commercial prosperity linked to the discovery and retrieval of

Moving to Shreveport after World War I, Grabill set up a commercial and portrait studio on Milam Street. One of his first commercial endeavors was for the Shreveport Ad Club, and Shreveport Chamber of Commerce, taking photographs of public buildings, local businesses, and residential neighborhoods. These were used for promotional purposes, including a sleekly designed 1919 publication, "Shreveport, Louisiana–Center of the Greatest Combined Oil, Gas, Agricultural and Lumber Field in the World," published by the Advertising Club of Shreveport, and the new Commercial Review magazine [later Shreveport Magazine] published by the Chamber of Commerce.

Below: Morris & Dickson Co., interior view, 1919.

Photo By Grabill ~ 11

natural gas and oil in Northwest Louisiana, made Shreveport an appealing choice. Thus in 1919 the Grabills arrived in the city, rented a studio at 614 ½ Milam Street, and acquired a place to live in the 700 block of Delaware Street near the then rural village of South Highland. Fortunately, Grabill had his own work vehicle, a black Model T paneled truck that bore the name of his studio and carried the accompanying slogan, "Photographs Live Forever." Over the years he adopted a number of advertising catchphrases, including the one that often appeared on his photographs—"Photo by Grabill." Studio and commercial field photography characterized those early years of energetic commitment and work, not only for the oil industry but also for local businesses, and the Shreveport Chamber of Commerce. By the early 1920s it must have been clear to Grabill that he had indeed made the right choice to move to Shreveport, in fact, the city was poised to enter a decade that proved to be one of the most economically auspicious and progressive eras in its history.

Below: Alexander School third grade class, Miss Mary E. Murry, teacher, May 23, 1919. *Dillard P. Eubank Papers, Noel Memorial Library Archives.*

Left: Centenary College coeds on the steps of the Scottish Rite Temple, 1919.

Below: Line Avenue School, 1919, designed by local architect, N. S. Allen, the building is now part of the Northwestern School of Nursing. One of the first photos marked with the logo, "Photo by Grabill."

The 1920s

DURING THE 1920s Shreveport experienced a remarkably positive period of economic growth and community leadership, much of which was faithfully recorded by the Grabill camera. The Roaring Twenties in the city were politically led from 1922 to 1930 by Mayor Lee Emmett Thomas, and economically guided by a host of talented business leaders. Both politicians and community activists alike were increasingly convinced that Shreveport's time as a civic and commercial entity of singular importance had indeed arrived, ample evidence of which, incidentally, unfolded during the decade. Historically, both cotton and lumber had provided the port city its economic underpinnings, a circumstance that began to change in the first decade of the twentieth century with the discovery of vast underground reservoirs of oil and natural gas in northern Caddo Parish and, shortly thereafter, throughout much of the region. At the behest of various oil companies, Burch Grabill, ever the entrepreneur, capitalized on these developments and, with photographic paraphanelia in hand, traveled about the area diligently recording on film the

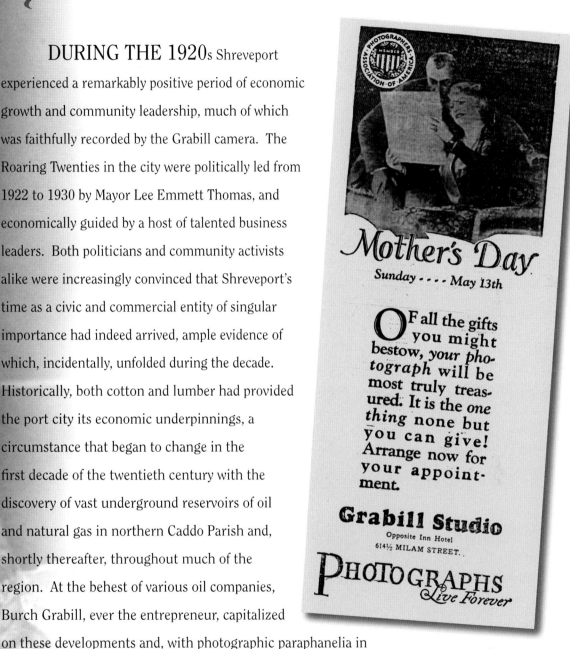

Above: Grabill Studio newspaper advertisement, 1920s.

Opposite: Georgie Agnes Harman (Chandler), Bessie Louise Stringfellow (Harman), and Bessie Harman (Barrow), Shreveport, La., ca. 1919.
Georgie Harman Chandler Collection, Noel Memorial Library Archives.

Although commercial ventures documenting the dramatic growth of downtown Shreveport, the oil boom, and the annexation and development of residential subdivisions occupied much of Burch Grabill's time, he still maintained a thriving portrait studio.

spectacle of what was a major oil boom. His work extended from the Caddo Field at Pine Island, to the deposits of Claiborne Parish in Haynesville and Homer as well as to sites in south central Arkansas at El Dorado and Smackover.

Also reflective of the prosperity of the era was a dramatic virtual citywide increase in building and construction. For the downtown area this meant the erection of a number of

Right: Clinton W. Longwill, secretary-manager, Shreveport Chamber of Commerce, ca.1926. *Shreveport Chamber of Commerce Collection, Noel Memorial Library Archives.*

Below: Group of young Shreveport society matrons, 1920s. *Shreveport Chamber of Commerce Collection, Noel Memorial Library Archives.*

Left: Fred Wappler and Ed Dickerson with prize catch, 1920s. *Georgie Harman Chandler Collection, Noel Memorial Library Archives.*

Photo By Grabill ~ 17

new office buildings which by the mid-1920s included the Ardis, Slattery, and Giddens-Lane. Also built during this decade were both the Washington and Jefferson Hotels, Feibleman's Department Store, the Selber Brothers Building, a new Y.M.C.A. at the corner of McNeill and Travis Streets, the Strand Theatre, and a replacement for the nineteenth-century Caddo Parish Courthouse which had stood since 1891. With the increasing help of his younger son Bill, this growth surge was actively recorded by Grabill as he operated out of his Milam Street Studio.

Burch Grabill was also very much involved in documenting the suburban effects

Right: The Inn Hotel, café and barber shop, 621 Milam Street, ca. 1920.

Below: Scottish Rite Cathedral, 725 Cotton Street, ca. 1920. Built in 1917, and designed by architects Edward F. Neild and Clarence Olschner in the Neo-Classical style.

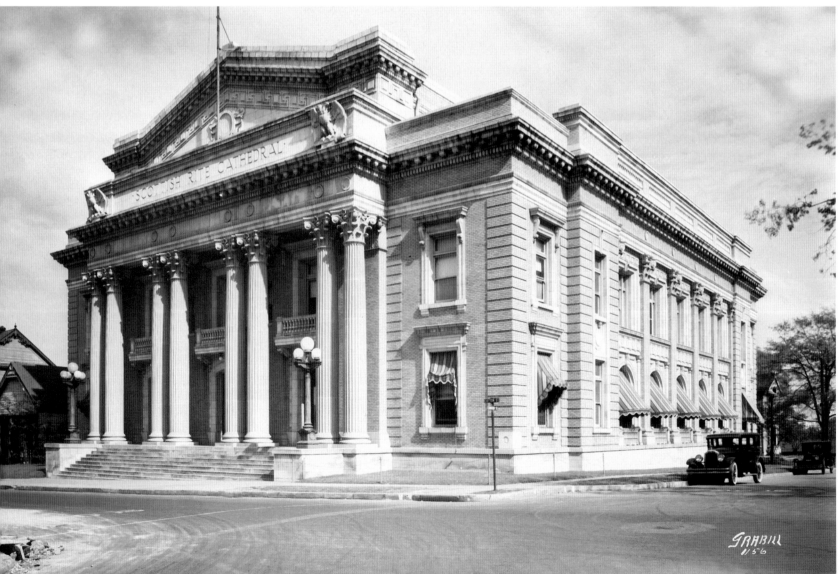

of the city's geographic expansion as its boundaries spread to the north, west, and south. Beginning in 1922, the western limit of the city was extended to Jewella Avenue and southward to Midway Street. Before the twenties were over, further southerly expansion included the 1927 annexation of the small towns of Cedar Grove and South Highland as well as most of the area now known as Broadmoor. Grabill's residential photography captured not only the growth in these new city acquisitions but also the construction of a number of stately homes and mansions along Fairfield Avenue, especially north of Kings Highway. Other noteworthy aspects of city life that Grabill managed to record on film included agricultural displays at the Louisiana State Fair, the aftermath of the multi-block Allendale fire of September 1925, and various phases in the construction of the Cross Lake Dam, which was finally completed in January 1926.

Thanks primarily to the work of the Grabill Studio, this extraordinary decade of growth and prosperity, one of the most impressive in Shreveport's municipal and economic history, has been preserved in photographs which continue as a source of information and fresh insights into the 1920s.

Below: Highland Sanitarium, northwest corner Highland Avenue and Marshall Street, ca. 1920. Opened June 18, 1917, designed by architect Clarence King.

162

YOUREE HOTEL

Left: Travis Street looking west from Market Street. Youree Hotel in foreground on left, First Presbyterian Church on right, ca. 1920.

Above: Neighborhood construction looking north from Village water tower.

Right: Fairfield Avenue looking south from Delaware.

Below: Delaware, 900 to 800 blocks, looking east.

Above: Milam Street, 700 block, ca. 1920.

Photo By Grabill ~ 23

Above: F. W. Woolworth Co., 500 block Texas Street, 1920s.

Right: Ida, Louisiana high school, 1920s. *Caddo Parish School Board Collection, Noel Memorial Library Archives.*

Ida High School before 1928

Below: Passover Seder, basement social hall, B'nai Zion Temple, 802 Cotton Street, ca. 1921.

Left: Youree Hotel, 406 Market Street, 1920s.

Below: Central Fire Station, 801 Crockett Street, opened Dec. 30, 1922. *Shreveport Chamber of Commerce Collection, Noel Memorial Library Archives.*

Photo By Grabill ~ 25

Right: Jefferson Hotel, 900 block Louisiana Street, just after opening ca. 1923.

Below: Commerce Street, 600 block, ca. 1920.

Text written on photo:
ALLENDALE
BINSON-SLAGLE LBR Co
WESTERN AVE + ANNA
CURTIS JN-4 airplane
PHOTO BY GRABILL K1434½
BY B.E. GRABILL 1924

Above: Aerial view of Allendale taken by Burch Grabill, 1924. Burch was never as fond of flying as was his son, Bill. By the late 1920s much of the aerial photography was being done by the teenaged Grabill. Note Allendale School on Pierre Avenue at upper left.

Left: J. A. Thigpen home, 2124 Fairfield Avenue, an excellent example of the Mediterranean Revival style popular in the eary twentieth century, ca. 1923.

Right: Well-known evangelist, Billy Sunday, wows the crowd during a Shreveport revival, March 23, 1924.

Right: Y.M.C.A., corner McNeill & Travis Streets, 1925. Designed by the architectural firm of Peyton & King in the Mediterranean style, the building featured an interior courtyard. *Shreveport Chamber of Commerce Collection, Noel Memorial Library Archives.*

Below: Corner of Texas and Market Streets, ca. 1925.

#1103
ALLENDALE-FIRE
9-5-25

Left & Below: The Allendale fire started Sept. 4, 1925 in the bathroom of the O. Childress residence at 1535 Garden Street. Because of difficulties with outlets and water mains from the city pumping station, virtually no water was available to the Shreveport Fire Department. One hundred and ninety-six homes were destroyed, and 1,200 residents displaced.

Strand Theatre – A partnership of two sets of brothers, Julian & Abe Saenger and Harry & Simon Ehrlich, built Shreveport's spectacular movie palace, The Strand. The brothers purchased the land on the corner of Crockett and Louisiana Streets in 1919, one block from the Saenger brothers' original drugstore. Construction began in 1923 and the theater opened July 3, 1925. According to the <u>Commercial Review</u> magazine, the Saenger-Ehrlich Enterprises had erected "the most magnificent theatre building in the entire South."

Above & below: The Strand under construction, March 27, 1924 and November 11, 1924.

Broadmoor **Golf Club.** Developed by A. C. Steere Co., the club opened in 1925 with an 18-hole golf course and clubhouse. In February, 1927 the club hosted a national open tournament that attracted professional and amateur golfers from all over the country to compete for $4,500 in prize money.

Broadmoor Country Club © Grabill 1304

Above: T. E. Schumpert Memorial Sanitarium, 941 Margaret Place, ca. 1927. The Shreveport Sanitarium was founded by local surgeon Dr. T. E. Schumpert in 1894. At the time of his death in 1908, it was willed to the Sisters of Charity of the Incarnate Word, who in turn named their new sanitarium in honor of Dr. Schumpert. It was dedicated on the third anniversary of his passing, May 16, 1911.

Above: Dodd College, the brainchild of Dr. M. E. Dodd, pastor, First Baptist Church, opened in the fall of 1927. The first catalog proclaimed the school "a standard junior college for girls exclusively," ca. 1927.

Below: Dixie Gardens Village, community center in foreground. Advertised as "where the country meets the city," it was conceived by A. C. Steere as a community of miniature farms. A gravel highway leaves Harts Island Road and winds through 84 plots that average 2 ½ acres in size. Shreveport magazine, April, 1928.

Below: Will H. Dilg League Clubhouse, ca. 1928. Dilg League Club, part of one of the first national nature conservation groups, worked to promote Cross Lake as a recreational venue. The Italia Moderna Society took over the property in the 1930s, renaming it the Progressive Men's Club. This structure was torn down in the early 1950s and replaced by a clubhouse that burned in June, 2003.

Left: Medical Arts Building, 634 Travis Street, opened 1928.

Below: Caddo Parish Courthouse, 501 Texas Street, ca. 1929. Built between 1926 and 1928, the third courthouse to stand on the site since 1859. Designed by Edward F. Neild, the Neo-Classical style was also used by Neild on the Kansas City, Missouri courthouse where it was much admired by future president Harry S. Truman. Truman later appointed Neild as supervising architect for the White House renovation project and to design the Truman Library in Independence, Missouri. *Shreveport Chamber of Commerce Collection. Noel Memorial Library Archives.*

Louisiana State
Fair–A mainstay
of the Louisiana State
Fair, the displays of
the Conservation
Department
showcased the
natural resources of
the state. Exhibits of
local retail businesses
and manufacturers
were for many years
an important part of
the Fair festivities.

Below: Grabill's Louisiana
State Fair advertisement,
<u>Shreveport</u> magazine,
October, 1928.

Above: Gateway to the Louisiana State Fair, ca. 1925.

Above: Bossier Parish agricultural exhibit, 1928.

Left: Shreveport Training School for Girls, Linwood Avenue near Kings Highway, ca. 1929. The school was established in 1906 by the Mother's Union as a refuge for girls from homes broken by death or other unfortunate circumstances. *Shreveport Chamber of Commerce Collection, Noel Memorial Library Archives.*

Below: A. C. Steere School, corner Youree and Ockley Drives, ca. 1929. Originally called the Broadmoor School, it was built in 1929, and a year after named to honor the memory of real estate developer and philanthropist, Albert C. Steere.

Above, right & below: Herman Loeb's Southern Hide, Fur, and Cotton Co., 700 block Commerce Street, was a major Shreveport cotton factor. Founded just after the Civil War, the company operated as the Loeb-Walker Co. through the 1950s.

Above & below: Haynesville, Louisiana oil tank farm, ca. 1922.

Oil and Gas–The first oil well in Caddo Parish produced 5 barrels on March 28, 1905, and the Caddo-Pine Island Field was up and running. By 1908 Oil City was a tent boom town. The early 1920s brought new fields discovered in Haynesville, Homer, Benson, Shongaloo, Bellevue and El Dorado, Arkansas. In 1929, petroleum refining was Shreveport's major industry. The Louisiana Oil Refining Corporation, with plants in Bossier and Shreveport, was probably the largest and best-known refinery. Between 1905 and 1960, 12,164 wells were drilled in Caddo and Bossier Parishes.

Above: Grabill's oil field photograph advertisement, <u>Shreveport</u> magazine, April, 1930.

Left: Haynesville, Louisiana at the beginning of the oil boom, ca. 1920.

Above: Bull Bayou Field, ca. 1919.

Right: El Dorado, Arkansas oil field, ca. 1922.

Below: Louisiana Oil Refining Corporation, Bossier Parish Field, ca. 1920.

Above: Union Refining and Pipeline Company, Oil City, Louisiana, 1920s.

Left: Northwest Louisiana oil field, ca. 1920.

Below: Oil field storage tanks, Homer, Louisiana, 1920s.

Right: Louisiana Oil Refining Corporation, northeast corner of Jordan Street and Fairfield Avenue, 1920s.

Right & below: LORECO Service Stations, Shreveport, Louisiana, 1920s.

Left: Standard Oil Company plane on Cross Lake.

Left & below: Arkansas Louisiana Pipeline Company distribution center in Northwest Louisiana, ca. 1929. ALPC was a subsidiary of the Arkansas Natural Gas Corporation. In 1934 it was consolidated with Southern Cities Distribution Co. to form the Arkansas Louisiana Gas Co.

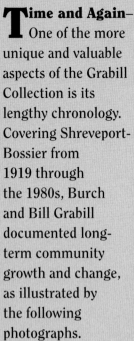**T**ime and Again– One of the more unique and valuable aspects of the Grabill Collection is its lengthy chronology. Covering Shreveport-Bossier from 1919 through the 1980s, Burch and Bill Grabill documented long-term community growth and change, as illustrated by the following photographs.

Right: Texas Street looking west, 1920s and 1950s.

James Lankford Collection, Noel Memorial Library Archives.

Above & left: Milam Street, 500 block, 1920s and 1950s.
James Lankford Collection, Noel Memorial Library Archives.

Right & below: Milam Street, 700 block, 1920s and 1940s. *James Lankford Collection, Noel Memorial Library Archives.*

Above, right & below:
Sidney Herold house, 820 Jordan Street, built in 1922. The Mediterranean-style home with Spanish tile roof is shown under construction, just after completion, and just prior to demolition in 1978.

Above: Shreveport Choral Club, 1925.

Left: Shreveport Choral Club, ca. 1970.

The 1930s

THE 1930S WERE A TIME of transition and change for the Grabill family as well as the Grabill Studio. In 1930 its location was moved from Milam Street to more spacious quarters on the fourth floor of the Hutchinson Building on Texas Street, across from the Caddo Parish Courthouse. As for young Bill Grabill, he was busy as a full-time student at Centenary College from 1930 to 1934, and in shared duties with his father as newspaper photographers for the <u>Shreveport Journal</u>, a position which was continued into the early 1940s. As heir apparent to his father and the family business, he had become increasingly involved with its operation over the years, beginning as far back as early adolescence and continuing through his years as a Byrd High School student. In addition, Bill Grabill had developed a veritable passion for flying and aerial photography since his first plane ride, at age thirteen, given by local aviator Currey Sanders in 1926. It was his initial flight-photography experience, and ignited a fervor for flying that he retained throughout his life.

Both aviation in Shreveport and Bill Grabill had, in fact, come of age at roughly the same time, the late 1920s and early 1930s. A scattering of airfields began to appear in the Shreveport area during the 1920s, and by mid-1931, the city had its own

ANNOUNCING

•

To Our Ark-La-Tex Customers and All Those in Need of Photographs for Advertising

•

W. B. GRABILL

has taken charge of our Commercial and Aerial Photography Department.

Give Us a Phone Call on Any Contemplated Work

A Photograph Is Worth Ten Thousand Words!

GRABILL STUDIO

Fourth Floor Hutchinson Building. Take Elevator

Above: Grabill's advertisement, announcing W. B. Grabill taking charge of commercial and aerial photograph departments, <u>Shreveport Journal</u>, 1930s.

Opposite: Bill Grabill with studio truck, "Grabill Portrait and Commercial Photographs," 1930s.

Show Him a Photograph

PRESENT photographic proof of
your performance claims. Your
prospects accept without question a
story the camera tells. We photograph
anything, anywhere, any time

GRABILL STUDIO
614½ Milam Street
Phones: 2-2403; Res. 8-1403

PHOTOGRAPHS
Tell the Story

Right: Grabill Studio advertisement, ca. 1929.

Below: Grabill's aerial survey plane, 1930s.

airport in Agurs, a recently-annexed section north of the downtown area, close to Red River. Even earlier, perhaps the major event in local aviation history had begun to unfold with the December 4, 1928 announcement that Shreveport had won the competition with other cities for the establishment of a major Army Air Corps base. Work was begun on the military installation in December 1930, and formally dedicated as "Barksdale Army Air Field" some two years later on Thursday, February 2, 1933; incidentally, the program cover that day was graced by a Grabill photo. Both in the air and on the ground, Bill Grabill had been present to record most of the major phases in its construction.

Queensborough School, Room 5, Grade 5-A, 1950

Above: Queensborough School, Room 5, Grade 5-A, 1930.

Left: Municipal Auditorium, February, 1930. A billboard advertises the arrival of Roland Hayes, first black American lyric tenor to win acclaim as a concert artist. An international reputation made Mr. Hayes popular in recital halls, but racial barriers denied his dream of an opera career.

Below: Shreveport Fire Station No. 10, 763 Oneonta, 1929 American LaFrance fire truck in bay, ca. 1930. *Shreveport Chamber of Commerce Collection, Noel Memorial Library Archives.*

Above: KWEA radio orchestra, ca. 1930. KWEA, "The Voice of Shreveport," was one of the area's first radio stations. Started in the early 1920s by W. E. Anthony, it ceased broadcasting in 1932.

Below: Robinson Place, 900 block, ca. 1930.

By the middle of the decade it was becoming increasingly apparent that Burch Grabill was being seriously affected by ill-health. In 1935, the year before his death from kidney disease at age sixty-four, he had been honored by local Spanish-American War veterans as "Commander" of the Shreveport unit and subsequently given a military funeral following his death at the end of June 1936. At age twenty-three, Bill Grabill and his mother, who was now in her late fifties, assumed complete control of the family business, and shortly thereafter made another studio move to the Rendall Building, in the 500 block of

McNeill Street, a location still in the heart of downtown Shreveport.

Despite the slowed economy of the Great Depression, the Grabill Studio evidently continued to enjoy relative prosperity. Bill Grabill maintained his position as a photojournalist in the employ of the Shreveport Journal, and with the help of his mother, Maude, still continued the traditional Grabill

Above: St. Vincent's Chapel consecration, December 2, 1931. *St. Vincent's Academy Collection, Noel Memorial Library Archives.*

Left: Italia Moderna Base-ball Club, 1932.

Barksdale Field– On November 7, 1930 civic leaders signed the deed that conveyed 22,000 acres of land in Bossier Parish to the federal government to be used as an air base. Over the next two years the land was transformed from cotton fields to Barksdale Field. Formal dedication was February 2, 1933.

Right: Aerial view of Barksdale Air Field, ca. 1935.

Below: Barksdale Field Dedication Day, February 2, 1933.

commitment to a diverse photographic fare. His work included the usual portraiture and commercial photography, as well as photographic assistance in cases of litigation, and the occasional snapshot of a celebrity or public figure making a visit to the city. Also noteworthy was the appearance of a Grabill photograph (regrettably unattributed) in a March 1937 issue of <u>Life</u> magazine, of the New London school explosion in nearby Rusk County, Texas. In any case, as the decade drew to a close, another major event occurred in the Grabill family with the

Above & left: Barksdale Field housing, ca. 1934.

September 1939 marriage of Bill and Shreveport native, Dorothy Mading. In the years ahead they would raise four daughters and share the experiences of an increasingly busy Grabill Studio.

Below: Barksdale Field squadron, ca. 1934.

AT EASE.

Right: Lambert Landscape Co., office, display grounds and greenhouses, 1411 Claiborne Avenue, adjoining Forest Park, ca. 1934. *Shreveport Chamber of Commerce Collection, Noel Memorial Library Archives.*

Below: Line Avenue School Mardi Gras Court, 1934. Betty Sue Snyder, Queen; Camp Flournoy, King. *Line Avenue School Mardi Gras Collection, Noel Memorial Library Archives.*

Above: Centenary Football Field, Gents versus LSU play to a packed house, 1932. The school campus is located to the north of the stadium; the stadium itself was severely damaged by a 1940 tornado, and is the current site of the Centenary baseball field.

Left: Centenary "Gents" football team, ca. 1934.

Above: Centenary Kollege Kapers, 1934. The cast of a student variety show next to their tour bus. Begun in 1933 and primarily directed by faculty member Dr. S. D. Morehead, the collegiate entertainers visited numerous places in north and central Louisiana. They performed their "singing, dancing, skitting, drama acting, and 'swinging' to the tunes of the Kollege Kapers orchestra," as described in the 1939 Centenary yearbook.

Right: Centenary graduates, 1934, included William Grabill, fourth row, last person on the right.

Below: Centenary Beauties of 1935. Ben Bernie (center), nationally-known vaudevillian, band leader, radio and movie personality, who coined the phrase "Yowsah, Yowsah, Yowsah," was asked by the Yoncopin yearbook editor to select "Miss Centenary" 1935.

Above: Municipal Farmer's Market, 2135 Greenwood Road, 1938.

Left: Eleanor Roosevelt with Shreveport Mayor Sam Caldwell, March 10, 1937. Mrs. Roosevelt made two talks at the Municipal Auditorium. Schools were dismissed and thousands lined the streets to see the First Lady.

Below: Kickapoo Plaza Courts No. 4, corner Benton Road and Highway 80, Bossier City, ca. 1935.

KICKAPOO PLAZA COURTS
AMERICA'S MOST COMPLETE - CAFE, CABINS, SERVICE STATION
A PHONE IN EVERY CABIN
1 MILE EAST OF BUSINESS DISTRICT SHREVEPORT, LA. HWY 80
TRAILER CAMP ADDED SINCE PICTURE WAS TAKEN

Above: Goodrich Silvertown Store, corner Louisiana and Cotton Streets, ca. 1938.

Right: William C. Kalmbach home, 500 Sherwood Road, ca. 1938.

Early Aviation–Although airplane flights were seen over Shreveport as early as 1909, its aviation history essentially began in 1919 at the Fair Grounds with the founding of the Gulf States Aircraft Company. This short-lived venture which provided aircraft for flight demonstrations at fairs and other expositions, gave way in the 1920s to the establishment of a few simple airfields, most of which were located just beyond the city limits. One of the earliest was Steere Field, built in 1924 adjacent to Mansfield Road in the area now occupied by the subdivision of Sunset Acres; it continued to be used by crop dusters and private aircraft into the 1940s. Another was the Shreveport Airport, which was dedicated on August 5, 1928, and was located about five miles west of the city proper, in what is now the 4700 block of Greenwood Road. About two years later, another airfield opening occurred near the Texaco oil storage facility on Anderson Island. The Texaco Airport was extensively laid out on land that included parts of today's Shreve City Shopping Center, and existed for about a decade. Both of the airports nourished hopes of establishing themselves as local centers of commercial aviation, but such dreams were dashed with the official opening of the city's own Downtown Municipal Airport in Agurs on July 14, 1931.

Above & below: Texaco Airfield–these photographs provide various views of the Texaco Airfield on October 15, 1930, the day that airmail flights were inaugurated to and from the city.

Left: Texaco Airfield on October 15, 1930, the day that airmail flights were inaugurated. Some of the Texaco oil storage tanks are visible in the background.

Above, below & opposite, top: The Shreveport-Greenwood Road Airport was the setting for these flying enthusiasts.

Below: The Ryan B-1 monoplane was a sister ship to Charles Lindbergh's "Spirit of St. Louis." In July 1929 local aviators William Currey Sanders and Van Lear Leary attempted and failed to establish a new flight-endurance record. W. K. Henderson, owner of KWKH radio station, helped sponsor the attempt.

Van Lear Leary Materials, Noel Memorial Library Archives.

The 1940s

AMERICA'S ENTRY INTO the Second World War in late 1941 had temporary but important effects on Bill Grabill and the family business. Because of his skills as an aviator, the military quickly ushered the twenty-eight-year-old reserve pilot into duty as a flight instructor. Basic training took place at England Air Base in Alexandria, Louisiana, before Grabill began formal instructional duties for the Army Air Corps in Texas, both at College Station and Jacksonville. As was the case for many Americans, his war effort involved a momentary disruption of career, although in many ways, Grabill was much more fortunate than others. Able to periodically return to Shreveport, he could, at least on occasion, continue with certain commitments, while the portrait studio work was being primarily carried on by his mother, Maude.

Despite the limitations of time, Grabill was also able to begin a photographic assignment that helped define his career and eventually become a professional and economic mainstay for a significant portion of his life. Toward the beginning of the decade, the Louisiana Department of Public Works had become increasingly mindful of the necessity of obtaining a yearly photographic mapping record of the effects of the ebb and flow of the lower Red River. Evidently aware of Grabill's growing reputation as an aerial

Above: Bill and Dorothy Grabill in front of their home. Dorothy Mading Grabill was the mother of four daughters, and for many years an elementary school teacher at St. Mark's Day School.

Opposite: Texas Street, 500 block, ca. 1949.

photographer, the department urged him to enter the bidding process. His bid in turn was accepted, and in the fall of 1942, armed with a recently acquired and military designed Fairchild A3B camera, he went aloft to begin what essentially became an annual photographic posting for the next forty or so years. In the beginning, this demanding and arduous aerial endeavor consisted of carefully photographing, from an average height of approximately 15,000 feet, that portion of the river from the Arkansas border in the north to its southeasterly

Above: Bill Grabill, flight instructor, World War II, perhaps in Jacksonville, Texas.

Right: Shriner's Hospital for Crippled Children, Kings Highway at Samford Avenue, ca. 1940. The first Shriner's Hospital in the country was dedicated in Shreveport April 1923. This complex was razed in 1983 to make room for a new facility.

Below: T. H. Scovell Class, Masons in front of Scottish Rite Temple, 1940.

Left: Getting the right shot – Bill Grabill perches with his camera on top of a large industrial wire spool in front of his truck, ca. 1940.

Right: During World War II one hundred and thirty-one Shreveport businesses were awarded U. S. Treasury "T" flags. Representatives of the firms that qualified for the blue and white minuteman flag were commended by Mayor Sam Caldwell "for splendid cooperation in meeting the challenge to make Shreveport the first Treasury "T" city in the South."

Below: Kilgore, Texas, center of the East Texas oil boom, 1940s.

confluence with the Atchafalaya and Mississippi Rivers, a distance of some 325 miles. With the exception of only two years in which he was underbid, Grabill was involved in this yearly autumn venture from age twenty-nine to seventy-one; his last Red River flight for the state occurred in 1984. He later observed in an interview that it took just two days of parallel flights down and back up the river to complete the task, but up to two months to develop the prints to the specifications of the Public Works Department.

70 ~ Photo By Grabill

Bill Grabill's attention was again drawn to the river in 1945. In the early spring of that year, the Ark-La-Tex began bracing for a major flood, the first to seriously threaten the area since 1908. The Red crested at Shreveport on April 7, and of course eventually ebbed, but not before Grabill, with camera in hand, took to the air. From Fulton, Arkansas to just north of Alexandria, Louisiana, he managed to take a number of visually stunning photographs of this epic event in local and area history. Nineteen forty-five was also noteworthy in marking the beginning of the post-war era, a period in which the Grabills made another studio move to the Simon Building in the 400 block of Texas Street. It was their last downtown change of address prior to their departure to the suburbs in the early 1950s.

Although the Grabill photographic portfolio that emerged from the 1940s was by necessity limited, it nevertheless reflected what had come to be, and would remain, a defining professional characteristic–a varied and eclectic assortment of images. It included, among others, the usual

Above: Jack Dempsey (third from left), world heavyweight boxing champion, 1919-1926, visited Shreveport in the early 1940s. This photograph shows Dempsey in his U. S. Coast Guard uniform, visiting with locals.

Below: Pittsburgh Plate Glass Company, 525 Cotton Street, ca. 1943.

photographs of commercial developments, a snapshot of former heavyweight champion Jack Dempsey on a visit to the city, a Masonic graduation exercise, and an aerial view of the initial phase of construction of the Hirsch Memorial Coliseum in the late 1940s. As the decade drew to a close and the economic promise of the fifties loomed ahead, the Grabills were set to make a major change not only in studio location but also in their growing family's place of residence.

Right: Natchitoches, Louisiana.

Below: Fulton, Arkansas.

Opposite: Jefferson, Texas.

All: *U. S. Army Corps of Engineers Red River Collection, Noel Memorial Library Archives.*

Red River Flood, 1945–Heavy rains in March 1945 caused disastrous flooding in Arkansas, Texas and Louisiana. Over a ten-day period the Red River and its tributaries crested from Fulton, Arkansas (April 2), down to Alexandria, Louisiana (April 13). Record-breaking high water marks were set on the Red, Sulphur, and Cypress Rivers. These photographs show flooding at Fulton, Arkansas (April 2), Jefferson, Texas (April 2) and Natchitoches, Louisiana (April 10).

74 ~ *Photo By Grabill*

Above, left & below: Downtown Municipal Airport, dedicated in 1931. The original terminal building was demolished in July, 1971. The old Downtown Airport site continues to serve the interests of private aviation. These photographs date from the 1940s.

Above: Construction on Hirsch Memorial Coliseum, Louisiana State Fairgrounds, began in 1947, but due to a lack of funds, was not completed until 1954. Aerial view, ca. 1948. *Louisiana State Fair Collection, Noel Memorial Library Archives.*

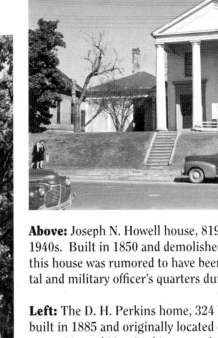

Above: Joseph N. Howell house, 819 Spring Street, 1940s. Built in 1850 and demolished in the 1950s, this house was rumored to have been used as a hospital and military officer's quarters during the Civil War.

Left: The D. H. Perkins home, 324 Wyandotte, was built in 1885 and originally located on Stoner Avenue. Mr. and Mrs. Perkins moved and restored the home in 1939. This photograph probably dates to the late 1940s.

Below: J. C. Penney Company, 400 block of Texas Street, late 1940s.

The 1950s *through* The 1980s

THE TEN TO FIFTEEN YEAR period following World War II proved to be, like the 1920s, another golden economic era in Shreveport history. In the 1950s most important business and commercial interests, with a few exceptions, were still centered and thriving in the downtown area. One of these exceptions was the Grabill Studio, which had relocated to the suburbs by 1951. Its new home was a green, multi-storied, frame house that stood on the northeast corner of Kings Highway and Samford Avenue. It was the studio's last move and, in retrospect, a commercial harbinger of the exodus to the surrounding city that occurred shortly after the fifties came to an end.

Early in the decade, Bill Grabill was adjusting not only to a new business address but also to a new family home. Since patriarch Burch Grabill and family had settled in Shreveport in 1919, they had always resided on Delaware Street in South Highlands. This changed between 1952 and 1953 with the move to a much larger two-story residence on nearby Unadilla Street. Maude Grabill, studio co-owner and professional helpmate to her son, continued to live in the original family dwelling until she was

Above: Bill and Dorothy Grabill at home, 575 Unadilla, 1960s.

Opposite: Bill Grabill with aerial survey plane, ca. 1950.

Photo By Grabill ~ 79

felled by a stroke in 1954. Shortly thereafter it was necessary for her to be moved to the Gowen Sanatorium on Line Avenue, where she eventually died in July 1955.

This last phase of Grabill's career would eventually cover an era which extended from the 1950s to the twilight of his professional life in the 1980s, a time of significant physical, economic, and social change in city history. Soon to disappear were such familiar downtown landmarks as First Baptist Church on Travis Street, as well as Union Station, a railroad passenger terminal on Louisiana Street, which had served Shreveport since the late 1890s. A new municipal airport on Hollywood

Above: Grabill Studio, 1256 Kings Highway, 1960s.

Below: Aerial view of downtown Shreveport, First Baptist Church, Travis Street, ca. 1950.

Left: Shreveport Chamber of Commerce Goodwill Tour, April 18-20, 1950. *Shreveport Chamber of Commerce Collection, Noel Memorial Library Archives.*

Below: Aerial view, Veterans Hospital, soon after completion, ca. 1950.

Avenue replaced its Airport Drive predecessor in July 1952 and in turn was superseded by another proximate terminal in the fall of 1971. Prior to the late 1960s, the Commerce Street riverfront remained as it had been for decades, an economically underdeveloped section of delapidated warehouses, a shantytown, and a few prosperous businesses; included

Above, right: "Greater Shreveport Airport," soon after opening in 1952.

Below: Shreveport Regional Airport, after the new terminal opened in 1971.

in this latter category was perhaps its best known attraction, the restaurant cuisine prepared by famed local chef Ernest Palmisano. In its immediate future, great change was in store for this once forgotten and long-neglected part of Shreveport.

As the city population continued to increase (from 127,206 in 1950 to 205,820 in 1980), new public schools which reflected this growth began to be built. They included such secondary facilities as Woodlawn (1960), Captain Shreve

Above & left: Ceremony and events celebrating the premiere of the movie "12 O'clock High" at the Strand Theatre, 1952. Shreveport Mayor Clyde Fant, third from left.

Below: Shreveport riverfront showing Texas Street Bridge, 1955.

Above: "Hale Boggs for Governor," headquarters, corner of Market and Milam Streets, Continental American Bank Building, 1952. Boggs was a U. S. Representative from Louisiana, 2nd District, 1941-43 and 1947-71, when he disappeared on a campaign flight from Anchorage to Juneau, Alaska, Oct. 16, 1972.

(1967), and Northwood (1967). In higher and professional education in Shreveport, the same decade witnessed the establishment of branches of LSU and Southern University, and the opening within the state of a second LSU School of Medicine which began instruction in the fall of 1969. New construction was by no means limited to academic institutions. Surely the greatest highway project in regional and city history, Interstate-20, was begun at the very end of the 1950s and continued throughout the early

1960s. Bill Grabill photographed its progress from the Texas border through Shreveport, across Red River and on to the east. Also caught by the Grabill camera during the following decade were various phases in the demolition and clearing of the grounds of the old St. Vincent Academy. Mall St. Vincent was subsequently built on that Fairfield area site and officially opened in early 1977.

Despite the fact that by 1980 Grabill was in his late sixties, he continued his work in aerial surveying and photography, although a year later, in 1981, he ceased the public listing of the Grabill Studio at its 1256 Kings Highway address. His last Red River survey for the state came three years later. The mid-1980s

Above: Long-time Shreveport chef, Ernest Palmisano, opened Ernest's Supper Club, 516 Commerce Street in 1965.

Left: Five hundred block of Commerce Street showing Ernest's, 1965.

Below: Popular local bandleader, Sammy Wimbish (left) with his orchestra, was signed to play for the Bob Hope Show at the Louisiana State Fair in October, 1966, when Hope's usual band, Les Brown and His Band of Renown, was unable to make the trip.

Above: Northwood High School prior to opening, 1967.

also brought personal challenge to the Grabill family as Grabill's wife, Dorothy, began to experience a marked decline in health. In December 1987, after a prolonged illness, this mother, former school teacher, and wife of forty-eight years, died at age seventy.

Bill Grabill's last years were spent at his home on Unadilla, where he enjoyed both the comfort of his remaining family and more than an occasional excursionary flight. In

Right & below:
Western Electric site. Groundbreaking for the plant on Highway 171 South was held May 3, 1965. The plant opened in January, 1967 with over 1,000 employees.

the late 1980s, this somewhat laconic and mild-mannered individual, had suffered the dismaying and acute disappointment of finding his old Kings Highway studio, now the property of the state and standing squarely in the path of Interstate-49, prematurely demolished. The fiasco resulted from a communication mixup in a previous agreement, with the result that, in a veritable instant, hundreds of his photographic negatives and older equipment were lost forever. According to him when he arrived that day, his former studio "was a pile of dust."

Never officially retired, Bill Grabill characterized his working status in March 1993, less than a year before his death, as "semiretired, I just work for the law firms now," he stated. Approximately ten months later, Grabill passed away on January 9, 1994. Following his death, there were numerous public tributes expressing appreciation for the lives of both Bill Grabill and his father Burch, all of them acknowledging an awareness that this father and son had bequeathed to Shreveport and Northwest Louisiana a priceless legacy of photographic images of this area's history.

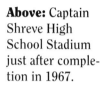

Above: Captain Shreve High School Stadium just after completion in 1967.

Left: Airline Shopping Center, 2325 Airline Drive, ca. 1968.

Below: Cotton's Holsum Bakery, Samford Avenue, using newly installed Webline conveyors, ca. 1968.

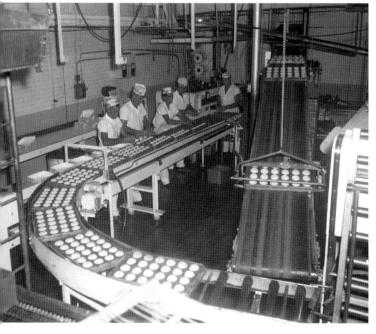

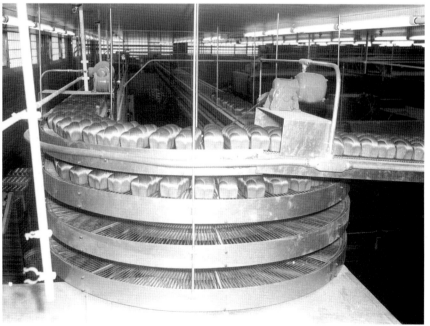

Photo By Grabill ~ 87

Above: Line Avenue, Byrd High School aerial view, late 1960s.

Above & left: Kelly's Truck Stop, I-20 at Highway 80, Greenwood, Louisiana, 1970.

Above: Texas Street, 400 block, showing construction next to the Post Office, advertising Shreveport, "City on the Grow," ca. 1970.

Left: Flag Island, Hodges Gardens, ca. 1970. Hodges Gardens, the largest privately owned horticultural park in the country, opened to the public in 1956. Flag Island, a memorial to the Louisiana Purchase, measures 110' x 60', and contains a large terrazzo map of the U. S. Flanking the map are 18 flags–five of the ten government standards and 13 of the states carved out of the territory.

Above: Aerial view of LSU Medical Center, ca. 1970s.

Above: Additional two-lane span of the Shreveport-Barksdale Bridge under construction, March 1971.

Right: Shreveport-Barksdale Bridge under construction, January 1971. This view is looking east from the center of the bridge.

Photo By Grabill ~ 89

Above: Louisiana Downs under construction, Feb. 20, 1973.

Right: Louisiana Downs after completion, ca. 1975.

Louisiana Downs–A crowd of over 25,000, including actor Burt Reynolds, was on hand for opening day at the races, Oct. 30, 1974. The thoroughbred track, built at a cost of over $20 million, opened amid both controversy and acclaim. The location, bordering Highway 80 East and I-20, brought the track to within and hour or two of more than a million potential racing fans.

Above: Mosher Steel Company of Louisiana, 6301 Linwood Avenue. Steel workers on strike, 1974.

Left: Centenary College, aerial view showing newly constructed Gold Dome, 1974.

Above: These images of Red River are good examples of Bill Grabill's aerial surveying photography. Although most of his photographs of the river were done for the state, these two were part of a series taken for the private sector in 1974, of a relatively undeveloped parcel of land in Bossier City.

Above & right: Libby Glass, 4302 Jewella Avenue, began operating as a division of Owens Illinois in 1973. The view at right also shows Atlas Refinery in foreground. Both photographs ca. 1976.

Below: Willis-Knighton, aerial view of $12 million expansion program featuring a radically designed coronary and intensive care unit, and an emergency department capable of handling 3,000 cases per month. ca. 1976.

Mall St. Vincent–St. Vincent's Mall opened February 2, 1977, anchored by an existing Sears store on one end and Palais Royal on the other, with room for 60 additional shops and a cinema. The ribbon was cut by Sister Marietta Welsh of the Daughter's of the Cross, Mother Superior of St. Vincent Convent.

Left: Mall St. Vincent under construction, 1976.

Below: Mall St. Vincent after completion, 1977.

Right: East Ridge Country Club, late 1970s.

Below: Aerial view of Bossier City, 1985, one of the last known Grabill aerial photographs.

Above: Bill Grabill about to go up on an aerial shoot.

Below: Bill Grabill poses with one of his father's old cameras. From a portrait in the background, Burch Grabill seems to watch.

Above: Bill Grabill looks over old prints and camera equipment, probably at his Kings Highway studio.

Index